EYE-LOOK
Picture Games

Look and Remember

A Photo Memory Game

by Kristen McCurry

CAPSTONE PRESS
a capstone imprint

A+ books are published by Capstone Press,
1710 Roe Crest Drive, North Mankato, Minnesota 56003.
www.capstonepub.com

Books published by Capstone Press are manufactured with paper
containing at least 10 percent post-consumer waste.

Library of Congress Cataloging-in-Publication Data
McCurry, Kristen.
  Look and remember : a photo memory game / by Kristen McCurry.
     p. cm. (A+ books. Eye-look picture games)
  Includes bibliographical references.
  Summary: "Simple text invites reader to recall details from full-color
photos"—Provided by publisher.
  ISBN 978-1-4296-7548-2 (library binding)
  1. Picture puzzles—Juvenile literature. I. Title.
  GV1507.P47M376 2012
  793.73—dc23   2011043260

Credits

Jeni Wittrock, editor; Tracy Davies McCabe, designer; Marcie Spence, media
researcher; Laura Manthe, production specialist

Photo Credits

Alamy Images: CLEO Photo, 4 (bottom left), 13, StudioSource, 3 (right), 25;
Capstone Studio: Karon Dubke, cover; iStockphoto: Fertnig, 31; Shutterstock:
Alexander Ishchenko, 17, Anatoliy Samara, 21, Bochkarev Photography, 15, Cheryl
Casey, 23, Igor Kovalchuk, 4 (top left), 29, Jennifer Pavelski, 27, Kesu, 4 (bottom
right), 7, matka_wariatka, 3 (left), 11, Noam Armonn, 4 (top right), 9, Thomas M
Perkins, 19, Vladimir Mucibabic, 5

Note to Parents, Teachers, and Librarians

The Eye-Look Picture Games series supports national math standards related to grouping, sorting,
and abstract reasoning, and national language arts standards related ot the use of comparisons
and analogies. The images support early readers in understanding the text. The repetition of words
and phrases helps early readers learn new words. Early readers may need assistance to read some
words and to use the Read More and Internet Sites sections of the book.

Printed in the United States of America in North Mankato, Minnesota.
102011   006405CGS12

Remember It!

How good is your memory? Do you remember the clothes you wore yesterday? How about what you ate for breakfast last Tuesday?

This book is a memory game. Look closely at each photo. Then turn the page to see how good your memory really is. You might be surprised at what you remember—and what you don't!

See the answer key on page 31 to check your answers.

At the Playground

What season of the year is it?

Is the girl holding on to the swing?

What color ties are holding her pony tails?

Is it sunny or cloudy?

Beautiful Butterflies

How many butterflies are there?

What color is the butterfly in the middle?

Where is the smallest butterfly?

Where is the butterfly with green stripes on its wings?

What safety equipment is the girl wearing?

What color liquid is she working with now?

Which color is in the jar on the left?

How many jars are on the table?

In the Refrigerator

How many shelves are there?

Where are the eggs?

Which color pepper is in front?

Where are the grapes?

Game Night

How many players are there?

Which color pawns are the players using?

Which child is taking a turn—right or left?

What number is on the top card?

What holiday is it?

What color napkin is under the chips?

How many drinks are on the table?

What vegetables are on the hamburger?

Bicycle Race

Who is sticking out their tongue?

Which numbers are on the bicycles?

Which riders' bikes have training wheels?

How many riders are wearing stripes?

Toy Time

How many children do you see?

Which animal is on top of the girl's head?

Where is the duck?

Which animal has a red nose?

Crazy Paint

Does the girl have socks on?

What colors of paint are on her cheeks?

How many jars of paint are in front of the girl?

What color paint jar is on the left?

What color is the bucket?

What kind of boat is on the water?

How many towels are there?

Where is the sea star?

Too Many Tools

What color is the peg board?

How many hammers are there?

What color is the triangle?

Where are the screwdrivers?

Fun Fair Food

What color is the word "Ice Cream" on the sign?

How many people are buying ice cream?

Where is the plant?

What picture is on the purple flag?

How many fish are there?

What color eyes does the yellow fish have?

Which fish is the smallest?

Where is the yellow fish?

So are you a memory champ yet? Anyone can become one! The secret is to take notice. Look at the details. Tell yourself what you're seeing. Imagine yourself there.

Now test your friends—and teach them these tricks so they can be memory champs too!

Answer Key
At the Playground: fall, no, green, sunny; **Beautiful Butterflies**: 9, blue and black, middle of the bottom row, top left corner; **Science Experiment**: goggles, blue, green, 4; **In the Refrigerator**: 3, bottom shelf, red, top shelf in the back; **Game Night:** 2, green and yellow, left, 2; **Let's Celebrate:** Independence Day, red, 2, tomato, lettuce, and onion; **Bicycle Race:** girl in the middle; 50, 56, 54; all; 3; **Toy Time:** 1, dog, top left, bunny with the scarf; **Crazy Paints:** no, yellow and red, 4, blue; **At the Beach:** red, sailboat, 1, between the shovel and the flip flops; **Too Many Tools:** white, 2, gray, lower left corner; **Fun Fair Food:** white, 2, in front of the ice cream stand on the left, ice cream cone; **Fish Friends:** 4, red, the pink fish, between the green and red fish.

Read More

Kalz, Jill. *An A-MAZE-ing Amusement Park Adventure. A-MAZE-ing Adventures.* Mankato, Minn.: Picture Window Books, 2011.

Kidslabel. *Toys: Seek and Find. Spot 7.* San Francisco: Chronicle Books, 2008.

Schuette, Sarah L. *Season Search: A Spot-It Challenge. Spot It.* Mankato, Minn.: Capstone Press, 2011.

Internet Sites

FactHound offers a safe, fun way to find Internet sites related to this book. All of the sites on FactHound have been researched by our staff.

Here's all you do:

Visit www.facthound.com

Type in this code: 9781429675482

Super-cool stuff! Check out projects, games and lots more at **www.capstonekids.com**